A Day with the Lord Jesus

ST. PISHOY KAMEL

Translated by

St. Mary and St. Moses Abbey

A Day with the Lord Jesus
By St. Pishoy Kamel

Translated from Arabic by St. Mary & St. Moses Abbey.

Designed & Published by:
St. Mary & St. Moses Abbey Press
101 S Vista Dr., Sandia, TX 78383
stmabbeypress.com

Contents

Introduction

In its style, this book provides a practical experience, whose words are not for reading only, nor are they to be used for superficial meditation, but they are for practical application, word by word, a step after another, in our daily life which we desire to live in union with the Lord Jesus.

In summary, this book offers an exercise in the direction of life we seek to live, as an easy way to spend our daily works with Christ, through Christ, and in Christ.

This life is not the affair of the human will alone, but rather it is the subject of the will of man, accompanied by prayer, and is moved by the mercy of God.

These pages are presented foremost to those who desire to spend a day in examining themselves by themselves, without human interference, and the Lord Jesus will Himself be the Teacher. And such a day of retreat and meditation can take place in solitude or stillness, or in the midst of surroundings and the daily preoccupations in our life. We do not want lengthy meditations, but it is sufficient that a person finds a few minutes at opportune times for reading such texts and applying them in our main works and our daily life. The structure placed here can be changed, but the main elements for meditation are presented in this book.

Some may be able to see the extent of the benefit of this method, which may be an extension of the same form which Jesus lived in His daily life.

People living alone are able to carry out this program. As for those who are married and those who live in a family, they may adopt the method that suits them. This book contains Scriptural words; let God Himself speak.

Communal Church worship of mysteries and rites was not mentioned here, for it is a fundamental and preliminary matter that we actually practice in our lives. All that this book tries to accomplish is to find an internal link between spiritual enlightenment in our internal life and our daily works.

This modest attempt to imitate Christ may seem to be a novel approach. Nevertheless, there are ancient, great fathers who had adopted it in their lives. For St. Basil stated, in his writings, that our works should correspond to the words of the Savior. Likewise, St. Gregory of Nazianzus wrote, saying:

And perhaps He goes to sleep, in order that
He may bless sleep also; perhaps He is tired
that He may hallow weariness also; perhaps
He weeps that He may make tears blessed.[1]

Such directions of our saintly Fathers are
sufficient to confirm the soundness of this book.

✠

Dear reader, this [aforementioned] was the
introduction the author wrote for the book. And the
Church, having presented this book to you, feels the
pressing need [for you] to experience the practical
life with Christ. The practical path is for you to
commit to memory the included verses and recite
them with delight in your daily life. The subsequent
step, which is of the work of the Holy Spirit, is to
begin recording new verses from the Scriptures, to
add them to what was included in this book. Begin
by immediately designating a notebook, to write
every verse that touches your practical daily life.

This book is a mere, simple specimen, that will
be, by the grace of the Holy Spirit, the first step for
the life of hope and rumination on the word of God.
Then you will say with the psalmist, "and in His
law, he meditates day and night" (Psalms 1:2). The

---

1   Gregory Nazianzen *Oration XXXVII. In Nicene and Post-Nicene
Fathers: Second Series* 7, P. Schaff, ed. (Peabody, MA: Hendrickson
Publishers, 2012), 338.

Holy Spirit is able to compel every reader to live the life of continual fellowship, which will turn into a fountain of water springing up into everlasting life.

A Day with the Lord Jesus

When I arise from sleep

"I lay down and slept; I awoke, for the Lord sustained me" (Psalms 3:5).

Before anything [else], let us give thanks to our God who covered us, preserved us and made us pass through this night in peace.

"I will arise and go to my father" (Luke 15:18).

Let us make our goal and direction [aimed] toward the Father throughout the day, so that we may dwell in His bosom. Let us go to Him as sinners on the path of repentance, and on our lips the words of the Prodigal Son, "I will arise and go to my father." In our going to the Father, we will find the Beloved waiting for us, knocking on our doors—waiting for our daily [morning] conversation.

9

> *"The voice of my beloved!... Behold, he stands behind our wall; He is looking through the windows, gazing through the lattice.... It is the voice of my beloved! He knocks, saying, 'Open for me, my sister, my love' ... My beloved spoke, and said to me: 'Rise up, my love, my fair one, and come away'"* (Song of Solomon 2:8—9; 5:2; 2:10).

This is an invitation to meet the Beloved, a meeting filled with all love and tenderness; an invitation to begin the conversation in the morning of every new day. For on every new day, we have an invitation and a meeting with our beloved Jesus.

> *"Very early in the morning, on the first day of the week they came to the tomb"* (Mark 16:2).

The Lord's resurrection from the dead very early in the morning, directs us early in the morning, with our thoughts and feelings, to the resurrected Lord. He overcame death and all the powers of evil, that we may come to Him, with the women, with our meager offerings of spices and ointments.

✠

❧ *When I wash my face* ❧

"Wash me thoroughly from my iniquity, and cleanse me from my sin.... Purge me with hyssop, and I shall be clean; wash me and I shall be whiter than snow" (Psalms 51:2, 7).

"Though your sins are like scarlet, they shall be as white as snow; though they are red like crimson, they shall be as wool" (Isaiah 1:18).

Water is a means of cleansing, and the cleanliness of the body is a symbol of the purity of the soul. And so the Lord grants us forgiveness of our sins and purity of our souls when we ask for these in faith, from the depth of the heart.

"I will wash my hands in innocence; so I will go about Your altar, O Lord" (Psalms 26:6).

After the forgiveness of our sins and repentance, we need to reach a state of purity of heart, that makes us worthy of being near to God in our prayers. For purity of heart is a necessary state.

"For as many of you as were baptized into Christ have put on Christ" (Galatians 3:27).

"[Are you able to] be baptized with the baptism that I am baptized with?" (Matthew 20:22).

11

Each time we wash with water, we remember God's mercy which renewed our souls in the Mystery of Baptism. The Mystery of Baptism is not only a cleansing from sin, but it also means that the baptized person puts on the Person of Christ and shares in His baptism; that is, he shares in His Passion[2] and patience.

✠

When I dress

"But when the king came in to see the guests, he saw a man there who did not have on a wedding garment. So he said to him, 'Friend, how did you come in here without a wedding garment?'"
(Matthew 22:11—12).

We are the heavenly King's guests, every day and always, invited to partake of the banquet of eternal life, which is the wedding feast of the King's Son and the human race. So do I have the wedding garment on, which makes me worthy of attending? And am I in a state of inner readiness?

"But the father said to his servants, 'Bring out the

---

2   I.e. suffering.

best robe and put it on him'" (Luke 15:22).

If we do not have the wedding garment, let us run to the heavenly Father, in reverence and humility, admitting that we have no wedding garment. The Father would then bestow on us a robe more glorious than what we had asked for, a robe which we did not expect. How magnificent a robe it is, for it is the best robe!

"When I passed by you again and looked upon you ... so I spread My wing over you and covered your nakedness.... And entered into a covenant with you, and you became Mine" (Ezekiel 16:8).

And here is God Himself, and not His servants, the One who covers me, covering me with His garment and by that I become His own.

"I will greatly rejoice in the Lord, my soul shall be joyful in my God; for He has clothed me with the garments of salvation, He has covered me with the robe of righteousness, as a bridegroom decks Himself with ornaments, and as a bride adorns herself with jewels" (Isaiah 61:10).

The glory of the Lord brings joy to my soul and gives it beauty. The wedding of the King's Son is my own wedding, and every time the light of a new day dawns, I say to myself, "Behold, your wedding day to Christ." And every day, my soul truly rejoices in this heavenly wedding.

"Also for Adam and his wife the Lord God made tunics of skin, and clothed them" (Genesis 3:21).

The mystery of the wedding garments is a heavenly mystery, concealed in the tunic of skin that the Lord God made for Adam, the first man. The Lord made it out of the skin of a slain lamb, a symbol of the Lamb of God, the Lord Jesus, who was slain for the salvation of the world.

✠

When I eat breakfast

"And looking up to heaven, He blessed and broke and gave the loaves to the disciples; and the disciples gave to the multitudes" (Matthew 14:19).

If we sit to eat our food, let us receive it from the hand of the Lord Jesus. Let us eat our food after the Lord blesses it. Since this is the first meal of our day, let us eat it while our eyes are fixed on high heavenward.

"I am the living bread which came down from

heaven. If anyone eats of this bread, he will live forever; and the bread that I shall give is My flesh, which I shall give for the life of the world" (John 6:51).

"He who eats my flesh and drinks my blood, abides in me and I in Him" (John 6:56).

"I am the bread of life. He who comes to Me shall never hunger, and he who believes in Me shall never thirst" (John 6:35).

"Lord, give us this bread always" (John 6:36).

"Jesus stood and cried out, saying, 'If anyone thirsts, let him come to Me and drink'" (John 7:37).

Partaking of the Body and Blood of the Lord is an essential Food for our life. Likewise, the invisible nourishment on the Lord Jesus, in faith and love, is similarly an essential food for our spirits throughout the day. With this determination, we can make every breakfast and every meal a fellowship with the Lord Jesus, the Bread of Life.

✠

⟨•← *When reading the Bible* →•⟩

"But He answered and said, 'It is written, "Man shall not live by bread alone, but by every word that proceeds from the mouth of God"'" (Matthew 4:4).

As our bodies live by the bread of the earth, and our souls by the Body and Blood of the Lord, so too must we eat and live by the word of God.

"He said to him, 'What is written in the law? What is your reading of it?'" (Luke 10:26).

And in light of this saying, I turn to myself, asking: Do I read? What do I read? How do I read? With what spiritual readiness do I read?

"Then I took the little book out of the angel's hand and ate it, and it was as sweet as honey in my mouth. But when I had eaten it, my stomach became bitter" (Revelation 10:10).

We therefore need to eat the word of God, and with longing assimilate and digest it in the vessel of our life. The bitterness of the word of God in our stomachs is due to the fact that the word of God works against our carnal instincts and in the opposite direction with the worst of what is in our human nature.

16

But at the same time, it tastes sweet in our mouths, sweet to the good aspects of us, sweet to our tongue with which we express what goes on in our thoughts of good meditations.

✠

Morning prayer & meditation

"But you, when you pray, go into your room, and when you have shut your door, pray to your Father who is in the secret place" (Matthew 6:6).

"I will hear what God the Lord will speak, for He will speak peace to His people and to His saints" (Psalms 85:8).

"If He calls you, that you must say, 'Speak, Lord, for Your servant hears'" (1 Samuel 3:9).

The Holy Scriptures emphasize the importance of secret prayer, which occurs spontaneously and without an intermediary between the heavenly Father and His children. It is a dual entreaty and a dialogue, and not a one-sided monologue. It is not so much a supplication of man to God, as it is to listen to the voice of God and His guidance.

"My son, give me your heart" (Proverbs 23:26).

If I am able to give my heart to God, this [act] becomes the best prayer. It is a secret gift, without words, and is an introduction to contemplative prayer, which I can practice throughout this day, without saying anything. It is enough that I remain silent and give myself—my entire self—to God.

✠

Daily affairs

Managing Daily Works

"For I am also a man under authority" (Matthew 8:9).

"I am not worthy that You should come under my roof. But only speak a word" (Matthew 8:8).

"For Your name's sake, lead me and guide me" (Psalms 31:3).

"The Lord will guide you continually, and satisfy your soul in drought ... you shall be like a watered garden, and like a spring of water, whose waters do not fail" (Isaiah 58:11).

"Lord, what do You want me to do?" (Acts 9:6).

Surrendering to the Guidance to God

Ask of God a strict, precise direction in all the matters of your life, and receive from the hand of the Lord every morning a program for your daily work. However, you should record in this program [even] the utterly simple works which may appear to be unimportant: our conversations, our speeches, our meetings, and so on. Every day of our life, in which God takes control over our direction, is a gift we offer to God.

Obedience with Humility

Let us be careful lest our own wishes clash with His divine commandments, for it matters to us that we live in complete submission to the Divine direction, and this is better than that we only ask Him [to fulfill our wishes]. Let us cultivate ourselves in this obedience, which is part of the boundless obedience of Christ to the heavenly Father.

"Then I said, 'Behold, I have come ... to do Your will, O God'" (Hebrews 10:7).

"Our Father"

"In this manner, therefore, pray..." (Matthew 6:9).

"Our Father" reaches to the top in our lives when we say it in the manner intended by the Lord Jesus when He said, "In this manner, pray." I mean when we say it in perfect conformity, not merely by the words which the Lord said, but in conformity with the mind of the Lord Jesus when He said it. That is, we say it while our souls are in a state of utter submission and perfect dedication to God.

During work

"My Father has been working until now, and I have been working" (John 5:17).

"Son, go, work today in my vineyard" (Matthew 21:28).

"There are diversities of gifts, but the same Spirit. There are differences of ministries, but the same Lord.... who works all in all" (1 Cor. 12:4—6).

Every work, no matter how simple, whether as a street sweeper, a cook, or a student in school, is none other than part of the everlasting work of the Father, and the Son, and the Holy Spirit, and part of the work in God's Divine vineyard. It is part of the great service in the mystical body of Christ, which the Holy Spirit undertakes through all the existing talents.

"And let the beauty of the Lord our God be upon us, and establish the work of our hands for us; yes, establish the work of our hands" (Psalms 90:17).

God's hand guides and helps us in the work of our hands, as it worked in the house of the one from Nazareth. The humbler and simpler the beginning of a work is, the more God showers both it and us with His glory and beauty, so long as the work is in full submission to the Divine thought, and so long as the Lord Jesus is in our hearts and minds.

"Let this mind be in you which was also in Christ Jesus, who, being in the form of God, did not consider it robbery to be equal to God, but made Himself of no reputation, taking the form of a bondservant" (Philippians 2:5—7).

"For who is greater, he who sits at the table, or he who serves? Is it not he who sits at the table? Yet I am among you as the One who serves" (Luke 22:27).

Every work that we undertake is considered a service,

21

and this service makes us eligible to be servants according to the same fashion which the sacrificing Servant, the Lord Jesus, showed in serving the Father and the people.

Let us rejoice all the more for the service we do in secret, without seeking external fame.

⌣⌐

"In Your light we see light" (Psalms 39:9).

"And you shall know the truth, and the truth shall make you free" (John 8:32).

"However, when He, the Spirit of Truth has come, He will guide you into all truth" (John 16:13).

Intellectual[3] work has a divine character to it, so long as the purpose of this work is goodness. Those who practice intellectual works should do so with humility, seeking the help and guidance of the Holy Spirit in all their works, that they may be guided by His shining lamp. But they should not become enslaved by their intellectual works, to the point that they lose their freedom in Christ, and they should also fiercely resist every attempt to oppress the spirit and prevent it from being set free and released.

✠

---

3   Or: mental.

At noon

"Tell me, O you whom I love, where you feed your flock, where you make it rest at noon. For why should I be as one who veils herself by the flocks of your companions?" (Song of Solomon 1:7).

Noontime is a suitable and acceptable time to draw near to our Good Shepherd, that He may lead us to green pastures, to receive our food from His hands, for He is the one who leads us and feeds us.

"Then the Lord appeared to him by the terebinth trees of Mamre, as he was sitting in the tent door in the heat of the day. So he lifted his eyes and looked, and behold, three men were standing by him; and when he saw them, he ran from the tent door to meet them, and bowed himself to the ground, and said, 'My Lord, if I have now found favor in Your sight, do not pass on by Your servant'" (Genesis 18:1—3).

Noontime is the time of clear revelation; it is one of the moments of manifestation, in which the Father, and the Son, and the Holy Spirit pass by us; therefore, we say with Abraham, "If I have now found favor in Your sight, do not pass on by Your servant."

"Now Jacob's well was there. Jesus therefore, being wearied from His journey, sat thus by the well.

*It was about the sixth hour. A woman of Samaria
came to draw water" (John 4:6—7).*

When Jesus was wearied from searching for me for
a long time and to no avail, He went to wait for me
by the water from which I come to drink.

Lord, I have come to You, to listen to You and to
quench my thirst, there at the well of Jacob.

This refreshing meeting at midday—though for
a few minutes—has a great impact on our daily life
and the renewal of our thoughts.

✠

At mealtime

*"He said to them, 'Have you any food here?' So
they gave Him a piece of a broiled fish and
some honeycomb. And He took it and ate in their
presence" (Luke 24:41—43).*

We should not sit at the dining table unless we are
sure that our eyes are full of the faith that makes us
see Jesus sitting at the head of the same table.

Let us eat and drink in perfect union with His
eating and drinking when He was on earth, that we
may enter into the fellowship of His Father's glory

and may share in His service to His brothers on earth.

"They also gave me gall for my food, and for my thirst they gave me vinegar to drink" (Psalms 69:21).

This mindset is necessary for us during mealtime, that it may preserve us from the intemperance resulting from ravenousness and overeating and overdrinking.

"For I was hungry and you gave Me food; I was thirsty and you gave Me drink" (Matthew 25:35).

Every mealtime, let us remember the needy and the poor. Let us do what we can for them, and then ask the Lord to help them.

✠

At the afternoon rest

The Lord Jesus devoted periods for resting with His disciples from the manifold, serious work.

He left the multitudes and withdrew from them for a while, spending his time in meditation and solitude, in the service of animals and birds, entertainment with the children, participating in gatherings at home and leisure time. This is the rule for resting, placed for us in the Gospel.

Despite the advancement of urbanization and the change in circumstances, this rule, nonetheless, still has its enduring value.

Therefore, how do we spend our free time?

Can Jesus take part in our leisure time?

"And He said to them, 'Come aside by yourselves to a deserted place and rest a while'" (Mark 6:31).

"So why do you worry about clothing? Consider the lilies of the field, how they grow: they neither toil nor spin; and yet I say to you that even Solomon in all his glory was not arrayed like one of these" (Matthew 6:28—29).

"And He was there in the wilderness forty days, tempted by Satan, and was with the wild beasts; and the angels ministered to Him" (Mark 1:13).

"Then they brought little children to Him, that He might touch them; but the disciples rebuked those who brought them.... And He took them up in His arms, laid His hands on them, and blessed them" (Mark 10:13,16).

"On the third day there was a wedding in Cana of Galilee, and the mother of Jesus was there." (John

2:1—2).

"[Jesus] said to him, 'Zacchaeus, make haste and come down, for today I must stay at your house.' So he made haste and came down, and received Him joyfully" (Luke 19:5—6).

"The Son of Man came eating and drinking, and they say, 'Look, a glutton and a winebibber, a friend of tax collectors and sinners!' But wisdom is justified by her children" (Matthew 11:19).

✠

The burden & heat of the day

"But you are those who have continued with me in my trials" (Luke 22:28).

We are going through trials and will go through trials. Our trials and sufferings are nothing but a part of the Lord's trials and suffering in Gethsemane. This perspective would elevate our trials and sufferings to the most sublime of meanings. They would be a continuation of the Lord Jesus' sufferings and trials.

"And when Peter had come down out of the boat, he walked on the water to go to Jesus. But when he *saw that the wind was boisterous, he was afraid; and beginning to sink he cried out, saying, 'Lord, save me!' And immediately Jesus stretched out His hand and caught him, and said to him, 'O you of little faith, why did you doubt?'" (Matthew 14:29—31).*

We learn from these verses that we should not look to the tempter nor the temptation, but look to Jesus, to see only the Lord. This is the necessary condition for us to walk above the water of temptation.

"Have mercy upon me, O God, according to Your lovingkindness; according to the multitude of Your tender mercies, blot out my transgressions" (Psalms 51:1).

Even in the middle of the day in which we live with the Lord, sometimes we fall because of the weakness of our nature. When we fall [into sin], however, we should arise at once, and offer repentance to the Lord. The Lord's look to Peter who denied Him, made the disciple weep bitterly.

So let us meditate, brethren, on the meeting of the Lord's eyes, full of tenderness, with our eyes, during and after our falling [into sin].

"And Jesus said to him, 'I will come and heal him'" (Matthew 8:7).

"Lord, behold, he whom You love is sick" (John

11:3).

"By your patience possess your souls" (Luke 21:19).

In the ordeal of illness and its trial, the Lord Jesus is able to heal us.

We trust in God's power of healing;

We trust in His exceeding love for us;

We trust that He knows what is best for us.

If the Lord does not give us healing, despite our trust in Him, and our supplications and prayers, we should surrender the matter to the Lord. More so, we should give thanks and bless God's will.

"They said to Him, 'Lord, come and see.' Jesus wept" (John 11:34—35).

Jesus shares in our griefs. He weeps also for the sake of those He loved unto death when He was in the body on earth.

"When they heard these things they were cut to the heart, and they gnashed at him with their teeth. But he, being full of the Holy Spirit, gazed into heaven and saw the glory of God, and Jesus standing at the right hand of God" (Acts 7:54—55).

As for a person's trial—through opposition to one's opinion, grudges, and hatred from others—if the person can gaze into heaven at the moment of trial, the person will see the Lord Jesus, instead of turning to the persecutors. This is of the highest levels of heavenly mercy which is granted to us in the midst of the deadly upheavals of the world.

✠

In the midst of the world, with friends

"By night on my bed I sought the one I love; I sought him, but I did not find him. 'I will rise now,' I said, 'And go about the city; in the streets and in the squares I will seek the one I love.' I sought him, but I did not find him" (Song of Solomon 3:1—2).

Sometimes Jesus is hidden from us, and we labor in search of Him and [yet] do not find Him. We should go to others to find Jesus in their midst.

"After that, He appeared in another form" (Mark 16:12).

He was the gardener; He was the traveler on the road to Emmaus; He was the stranger who appeared to the disciples on the shore of the Sea of Galilee;

He was... But even His friends did not recognize Him at first glance.

The Lord Jesus intends to appear to us in "another form," in the form of those surrounding us, to make it easy for us to see Him, as one of those around us.

⌣

"Then the righteous will answer Him, saying, 'Lord, when did we see You hungry and feed You, or thirsty and give You drink? When did we see You a stranger and take You in, or naked and clothe You? Or when did we see You sick, or in prison, and come to You?' And the King will answer and say to them, 'Assuredly, I say to you, inasmuch as you did it to one of the least of these My brethren, you did it to Me'" (Matthew 25:37—40).

This is the mystery of discovering the presence of the Lord Jesus in our midst in our present time. This is our experience of the Lord Jesus, who is risen from the dead, in our present life. This is our present opportunity to feel the Lord's wounds, and to see the mark of the nails in people's lives, who are members of the Lord's body, those who are bearing the sufferings of this world.

⌣

"Then there appeared to them divided tongues, as of fire, and one sat upon each of them. And they were all filled with the Holy Spirit and began to speak with other tongues, as the Spirit gave them

utterance.... Everyone heard them speak in his own language" (Acts 2:3—4,6).

Likewise, every person who walks with the Lord and receives the Holy Spirit, can speak with many tongues. Not with earthly languages only, but he will speak with sensibility toward others, feeling their pain and sharing in their thoughts. He finds a way to everyone's heart, thus learning all their demeanors and temperaments.

✠

The ninth hour

"If anyone desires to come after Me, let him deny himself, and take up his cross, and follow Me" (Matthew 16:24).

What is this personal cross? Our feelings towards the cross should not be general or theoretical. What is that right determination and painful understanding which the Lord Jesus is demanding of us?

The purpose of this meditation is to help me find the Lord and receive Him. For although it is my personal cross, it is nevertheless a part of the cross of the Lord.

*"Greater love has no one than this, than to lay
down one's life for his friends" (John 15:13).*

Unconditional love requires of us:

First, to be ready to immediately die for others,
and to offer our life as a sacrifice for them.

Second, if we have no aspiration to die
immediately for others, it is no less that we die for
them gradually; that is to say, to take every step
in the spirit of sacrifice and mortification, whose
ultimate purpose is death.

There are no small crosses; it is, rather, a
single cross, that is, the cross of Golgotha. And
this means that we should practice all kinds of
small mortifications in the fullness of the spirit of
Golgotha.

*"I have been crucified with Christ; it is no longer I
who live, but Christ lives in me; and the life which
I now live in the flesh I live by faith in the Son
of God, who loved me and gave Himself for me"
(Galatians 2:20).*

The demands of unconditional love cannot be
fulfilled unless the Person of the Lord Jesus takes
our place, and is Himself the center of our prayers,
our will and our being. So we die every moment to
the "I," which is, the ego. That is, we are crucified

with Christ, so we receive a new life.

We are mistaken if we understand that Christianity is merely mirth and buffoonery. No! It is a crucifixion, but the joy of the cross is an invaluable joy.

Every day is like Great Friday before it becomes the day of the Glorious Resurrection.

"I now rejoice in my sufferings for you, and fill up in my flesh what is lacking in the afflictions of Christ, for the sake of His body, which is the church" (Colossians 1:24).

He suffered for us, so if we are crucified with Christ, we are also partakers of His salvific work. That is to say, we realize personally the sufferings of Christ in our body, which is a member in the mystical body of the Lord Jesus. The values of abandonment appear then in our life, like renunciation, asceticism, voluntary poverty, obedience, and chastity, all of which are an offence and insanity in the view of the world.

"For I am already being poured out as a drink offering" (2 Timothy 4:6).

If we offer ourselves as a sacrifice, we share in union with Christ in the offering of Himself as a sacrifice. So am I truly ready for that?

"...in his new tomb which he had hewn out of the rock" (27:60).

"I will put you in the cleft of the rock, and will cover you with My hand" (Exodus 33:22).

"He who dwells in the secret place of the Most High shall abide under the shadow of the Almighty" (Psalms 91:1).

The stillness, secrecy, and the hidden life with the Lord Jesus, as well as the life of contemplation—all these are within the reach of any one of us, even if it were for just a few minutes each day. These are the most valuable minutes in our life, in which we try to be nameless and unknown to others.

"For you died, and your life is hidden with Christ in God" (Colossians 3:3).

Let us share His tomb with Him, as in His crucifixion also.

Let us stand near the Lord Jesus, beside the Father, in silence and unity.

✠

❦ *The Evening Song* ❦

"And when He had sent the multitudes away, He went up on the mountain by Himself to pray. And when the evening came, He was alone there" (Matthew 14:23).

"I was mute with silence, I held my peace even from good; and my sorrow was stirred up. My heart was hot within me" (Psalms 39:2—3).

"And behold, the LORD passed by, and a great and strong wind tore into the mountains and broke the rocks in pieces before the LORD, but the LORD was not in the wind; and after the wind an earthquake, but the LORD was not in the earthquake; and after the earthquake a fire, but the LORD was not in the fire; and after the fire a still small voice. So it was, when Elijah heard it, that he wrapped his face in his mantle and went out and stood in the entrance of the cave" (1 Kings 19:11—13).

"Today, if you will hear His voice, do not harden your hearts" (Hebrews 3:7—8).

"You who dwell in the gardens, the companions listen for your voice—let me hear it!" (Song of Solomon 8:13).

"My beloved has gone to his garden, to the beds of spices, to feed his flock in the gardens, and to gather lilies. I am my beloved's, and my beloved is mine. He feeds his flock among the *lilies"* (Song of Solomon 6:2—3).

During this time, the quiet time of sunset, let us keep for ourselves a few moments with the Beloved, in which we meet with Him in enclosed gardens and listen to His calm voice.

✠

Supper with Christ

"Behold, I stand at the door and knock. If anyone hears My voice and opens the door, I will come in to him and dine with him, and he with Me" (Revelation 3:20).

"But they constrained Him, saying, 'Abide with us, for it is toward evening, and the day is far spent.' And He went in to stay with them" (Luke 24:29).

Sometimes, we ask Him that He may accept our invitation. And other times, He [Himself] comes forth to us. Let us have the desire of always dining with Him, as He too desires to dine with us.

"With fervent desire I have desired to eat this Passover with you" (Luke 22:15).

Christ's desire is not only to dine with us but also to partake with us in the feast of Passover. Therefore, every meal can turn into a spiritual Passover, into an inner nourishment from the Lamb who was slain for our sakes, and a commemoration of the Last Supper in the Upper Room. Every supper should have a holiness of its own because of these meanings.

"'If I do not wash you, you have no part with Me.' Simon Peter said to Him, 'Lord, not my feet only, but also my hands and my head!'" (John 13:8—9).

The washing of the feet is the prelude to the Lord's Supper.

At the end of the day, and before the supper with the Lord, we need to be purified from all the dirt and sins which defiled us throughout the journey of the day.

Let us look to the Lord Jesus Christ, with the eye of faith, girding Himself, pouring water from a basin onto our feet and drying them for us. He kneels at my feet, while it was I who should have fallen in contrition at His feet, weeping, as the sinful woman did.

"Now it came to pass, as He sat at the table with them, that He took bread, blessed and broke it, and gave it to them. Then their eyes were opened and they knew Him" (Luke 24:30—31).

My God, let every time wherein we break bread be a confession of Your presence with us.

Let us also remember that the breaking of bread should be with others—the breaking of bread, that is, almsgiving. For where there is giving and generosity, there also the Lord is present. And when we break [bread] for His sake, and give with Him, then we also receive Him in us and are fed on Him.

"Now there was leaning on Jesus' bosom one of His disciples, whom Jesus loved" (John 13:23).

Every period of time that follows the mystery of spiritual fellowship with the Lord is a truly blessed time. For during this time, I can lean on Jesus' bosom and exchange with Him words no one hears, a conversation that follows the Lord's supper, or say, mere silence, in which there is an experience of the mystical union with Christ.

✠

Gethsemane

"Coming out, He went to the Mount of Olives"

(Luke 22:39).

"For Jesus often met there with His disciples"
(John 18:2).

"Then He came to the disciples and found them sleeping, and said to Peter, 'What! Could you not watch with Me one hour?'" (Matthew 26:40).

Jesus would like to take us with Him to Gethsemane, if we desired that ourselves, in order that we take part in His keeping watch. Have we devoted one hour for that holy time to keep watch? If we are not able to do that, at the very least we should spend some spiritual time every day in Gethsemane.

"Father, if it is Your will, take this cup away from Me; nevertheless not My will, but Yours, be done"
(Luke 22:42).

Let us accept the cup and deny our will.

Let us cling to God's will, in perfect unity with Jesus. This is the fruit of the garden.

In order to have practical experience in this field, let us offer an acceptable worship to Jesus, during His sufferings while His sweat was falling down to the ground as drops of blood.

"Let them now make intercession to the Lord of hosts" (Jeremiah 27:18).

"Therefore He is also able to save to the uttermost those who come to God through Him, since He always lives to make intercession for them" (Hebrews 7:25).

The spiritual moments in Gethsemane are the best moments wherein we may offer our supplications, for our supplications become one with the Lord Jesus' supplications for the sake of the whole world, during His suffering. In this moment, there is no need for many words. Nothing is needed except that we become one with the Lord, and He will present all humankind's needs to the Father.

"And He bore the sin of many, and made intercession for the transgressors" (Isaiah 53:12).

A powerful intercession for the sake of sinners, for all the sins of the people that are committed during this night!

"Father forgive them" (Luke 23:34).

"Let my prayer be set before You as incense, the lifting up of my hands as the evening sacrifice" (Psalms 141:2).

Let us offer a sacrifice—offer ourselves to God before we rest for the night.

⟨⟨ *Removing our garments* ⟩⟩

"And they stripped Him" (Matthew 27:28).

Let us accept to be stripped of everything with Christ in His sufferings.

I surrender all that I have to my Savior.

I strip away everything from me, but do not go far from me, O my Savior.

✠

⟨⟨ *Sleeping* ⟩⟩

"Father, into Your hands I commit My spirit" (Luke 23:46).

I surrender, not only everything I have, but myself too, surrendering myself fully. This is the work of perfect trust. And with the last motion in our waking time, and before we fall asleep, let us utter the words which Jesus said during the sacrifice of the cross.

"Having said this, He breathed His last" (Luke 23:46).

42

Sleeping is, to some extent, a giving up of the spirit. My going to sleep is mystically connected to the death of the Lord Jesus, which is a sign established between us and Jesus. Giving up the spirit is not a mere event necessary to nature, but it is also a willful and filial substitution for a divine trust in sleep, as in death.

"But He was in the stern, asleep on a pillow"
(Mark 4:38).

Our sleep was blessed by the sleep of the Lord Jesus during His life in the flesh on earth. When I sleep, I partake with Jesus in His sleep. May the sleep of Jesus be our own sleep.

"I sleep, but my heart is awake" (Song of Solomon
5:2).

My heart awakes during sleep if I have surrendered it into the hands of the Lord.

"And at midnight a cry was heard: 'Behold, the bridegroom is coming; go out to meet him!'"
(Matthew 25:6).

"Watch therefore, for you do not know when the master of the house is coming—in the evening, at midnight, at the crowing of the rooster, or in the morning—lest, coming suddenly, he find you sleeping" (Mark 13:35—36).

If we wake up during the night, willingly or not, let us remember His coming, not only His Second Appearance full of glory, but also His appearance at the time of our death. Whenever I wake up, I come closer to that coming, the coming of the Savior. And perhaps I am very close to it.

I sleep, and this is a natural necessity, but my lamp should be cleaned and filled with oil like the wise virgins.

The coming of the Lord should be [expected] at every moment of our life; He comes, and comes at all times. He comes at the hour of our death; He comes now and always. So, am I ready for His coming at this very moment?

The One coming is not only the master of the house. He is the Bridegroom. He is the Beloved. Once again, He speaks of the strong relationship between Jesus and the soul as a marital relationship, because it transcends mere friendship. This is the great mystery of the spiritual life.

For this reason, we should await the coming of the Lord with longing. In that day, we will return to the Lord, and then all the voices of our longing will be silenced.

"Make haste, my beloved, and be like a gazelle or a young stag on the mountains of spices." (Song of Solomon 8:14).

"Surely I am coming quickly. Amen. Even so, come, Lord Jesus!" (Revelation 22:20).

On the Daily Canonical Prayers

In order to ensure the fulfillment of Christ's commandment that men ought to pray at all times and not lose heart, the Church divided the twelve hours of the day into six parts, and made for each daytime part a suitable prayer of psalms, a reading from the gospels, and a group of litanies. As for nighttime, the Church assigned for it one prayer at midnight, divided into three watches. With this, it became possible to fulfill the commandment of the Lord Christ to pray at all times, by practicing the seven prayers, each at its appointed time. These prayers, which are compiled in the Agpeya (the Book of Hours), essentially constitute the rite of prayer at all times, regulating life and sanctifying it through prayer, and an expression of the constant watching of the heart awaiting the happy ending with the coming of the Bridegroom, which emphasized by the Lord: "And what I say to you,

I say to all: Watch!" (Mark 13:37). For this reason, the Seven Hours of each day are concluded by the Midnight Prayer, as an expression of watching until the Bridegroom comes.

Appointed Times of Prayer

Prime Hour (6 a.m. or after waking up)

This hour corresponds to the Resurrection of the Lord early Sunday morning. Therefore, we say at its beginning "And rose from the dead on the third day, and raised us with Him." It is also accompanied by daybreak, for the light is a symbol of the Lord Jesus, the True Light. Therefore, we pray in the first litany, "O the true Light Who gives light to every man." We also pray in the second litany, "As the daylight shines upon us, O Christ Our God, the True Light, let the luminous senses and the bright thoughts shine within us, and do not let the darkness of passions hover over us." We also emphasize that the Lord Jesus is the beginning of every work throughout the day, and so we pray in the gospel, "In the beginning was the Word, and the Word was with God, and the Word was God. He was in the beginning with God. All things were made by Him; and without Him was not anything made that was made."

Third Hour Prayer (9 a.m.)

This hour corresponds to the hour of the descent of the Holy Spirit on the disciples on the day of Pentecost. We pray during the litanies, "Your Holy Spirit do not take away from us," "renew a steadfast spirit within me," and, "…a spirit of prophecy and chastity, a spirit of holiness." Then we pray, "Purify us from all defilement… grant us Your peace, and save us, and deliver our souls."

The Third Hour also corresponds to the trial of the Lord Jesus, for at this time, the Lord was brutally scourged 39 times for the sake of our sins, and a crown of thorns was placed on the most holy place—His head—for our thoughts and the evils of our minds. In this hour, the sentence of death by the cross was issued.

Sixth Hour Prayer (12 p.m. or at noon)

This prayer corresponds to the holiest hour of the day, when Christ ascended the throne of the cross—the hour in which the nails were hammered. In this hour, we pray, "Put to death our pains by Your healing and lifegiving passions, and by the nails with which You were nailed. Rescue our minds from thoughtlessness of the earthly deeds and worldly lusts, to the remembrance of Your heavenly commandments." For the cross is a means of transporting our thoughts to heaven.

We then contemplate the stretched-out arms on the cross and say thankfully, "You wrought salvation in the midst of all the earth, O Christ our God, as You stretched Your holy hands on the cross. Therefore, all nations cry out saying, 'Glory to You O Lord.'" "We worship Your incorruptible person.... For, of Your will, You were pleased to be lifted up onto the Cross, to deliver those whom You created from the bondage of the enemy.... We give thanks to You, for You have filled all with joy, O Savior."

In this hour, the gospel says:

Blessed are the poor in spirit—so that we humble ourselves before the Lord in His poverty.

Blessed are those who mourn—so that we may mourn over our sins.

Blessed are the meek—so that we learn how to treat our colleagues at work [with meekness].

Blessed are those who hunger and thirst—so that we always thirst to be in the presence of God.

Blessed are the merciful—so that we perform acts of mercy throughout the day.

Blessed are the pure in heart—so that we may keep watch over our desires, our greed, the thoughts of our heart, and may be cautious of hatred and anger.

Blessed are the peacemakers—so that peace may become our goal during work.

Blessed are those who are persecuted... rejoice and be exceedingly glad—so that we endure with our Lord who endured the shame of the cross without a cause.

You are the salt of the earth... you are the light of the world—so that we may remember God's purpose for our presence in our place of work, and may be wary of grumbling and fear, and may understand our mission in this place which may at times be tiresome. Our mission is to glorify the name of God by being salt and light.

Ninth Hour Prayer (3 p.m.)

This corresponds to the hour in which the Lord yielded up His pure spirit on the cross, saying, "Into Your hands I commit My spirit." In this hour we submit all the troubles of our day and all that we have into the hands of the Father.

Shortly before this hour, the Lord was pierced with a spear in His blessed side, so blood and water flowed from it, to encourage us to endure every reckless piercing from the world.

In it also the Lord was thirsty and said, "I thirst." He thirsted for our lost souls. This thirst encourages us to bear all thirst, privation, and fasting, in honor of this thirst. The Church commands us to fast until this hour during the Holy Great Fast and on Wednesdays and Fridays, in honor of the Savior's thirst.

It is also the hour in which our Lord promised the thief that he would be with Him in paradise. Therefore, we pray "O You who guided the thief who was crucified with You into entering the Paradise, do not neglect me, O Good One, nor reject me, I, the lost one."

Likewise in this hour, the Lord descended into Hades through the cross, "having disarmed principalities and powers, He made a public spectacle of them, triumphing over them in it" (Colossians 2:15), and restored our father Adam and his children to Paradise. Therefore, we pray in the absolution and say, "And shine upon us as You have shone upon those who were in the darkness of Hades, and restore us all to the paradise of joy."

We also remember the suffering Mother, Virgin Mary during this hour and pray, and say, "The world rejoices in receiving salvation, while my heart burns as I look at Your crucifixion which You are enduring for the sake of all, my Son and my God." For the sake of her love for us, we ask for her intercession.

As for the gospel of this hour, it speaks about the power and responsibility of the Lord Jesus, of feeding the multitudes that came to Him for the sake of their spiritual nourishment. The gospel proclaims that they all were filled, and twelve baskets were left over. This draws our attention to [the truth] that all the spiritual and material deficiencies in my relationships with others, can be perfected by the Lord Jesus, who satisfies all.

Vespers Prayer or the Eleventh Hour Prayer

This hour corresponds to the bringing down of the pure body of the Lord from the cross, in awe and reverence. It is the last of the images of the cross, on which the Lord endured the shame, despising it to the point of death. And it is an image of the love of the Lord for His own to the very end, even unto death. This, too, is the highest degree of sacrifice for the sake of man.

The setting of the sun indicates the setting of the sun of our lives. Therefore, the litanies remind us of the burden and heat and the temptations of the day. They then remind us of God's mercy which He showed to those of the eleventh hour just as to those of the first hour.

The reading of the gospel says to us that at sunset—at the end of the day—when the sick failed to cure their psychological, physical and spiritual illnesses, "all those who had any sicknesses with diverse diseases brought them unto Him; and He laid His hands on every one of them and healed them." This emphasizes that our healing is a pledge of the touch of Lord Jesus.

The psalms of this hour are greatly connected to the spiritual sunset.

"Woe is me! My sojourning was prolonged.... My soul sojourned a long time as a resident alien."[4] For all of life is a sojourning.

"I lifted my eyes to the mountains; from where shall my help come.... The sun shall not burn you by day,"[5] "our soul would have passed through a water that is overwhelming."[6] The whole day is an unending water, and God makes us pass through it.

"The snare was broken, and we were delivered."[7] For how many traps were broken around us, and we are unaware.

"Those who sow with tears shall reap with exceeding joy."[8] This is the joyful fruit for those who struggle spiritually.

Compline Prayer or the Twelfth Hour Prayer

This hour corresponds to the burial of the Lord in the tomb, and He was buried so that He may bury my sins with Him, and He entered the darkness of the tomb, which is full of the sins of humanity, so that He may illuminate it with His pure body.

Man's sleep is a symbol of death; therefore, the Church chose the prayer of Simeon the Elder for

---

4   Psalms 119:4–5 LXX, OSB.

5   Psalms 120:1, 6 LXX, OSB.

6   Psalms 123:5 LXX, OSB.

7   Psalms 123:7 LXX, OSB.

8   Psalms 125:5 LXX, OSB.

this hour: "Lord, now You are letting Your servant depart in peace, according to Your word; for my eyes have seen Your salvation." The desire of the faithful, who have seen the salvation of the Lord, is to sleep in the hands of the Lord and to commit their spirit into the hands of the Lord Christ—"into Your hands I commit my spirit."

One of the psalms of the Twelfth Hour emphasizes this truth, that the Christian would not see a peaceful sleep except after he finds a dwelling place for the Lord in his life. "I shall not enter my dwelling, I shall not recline on my bed, I shall not close my eyes in sleep nor my eyelids for dozing, nor give any rest to my temples, until I find a place for the Lord, a tabernacle for the God of Jacob."[9]

Sleep symbolizes the end of man's life. Therefore, it is good that a person examines oneself at the end of the day, praying with the litanies, "Behold, I am about to stand before the Just Judge terrified and trembling because of my many sins. For a life spent in pleasures deserves condemnation. But repent, O my soul.... But if your wicked deeds and ugly evils were exposed before the Just Judge, what answer would you give?"

Midnight Prayer

We start the Midnight Prayer by saying, "Arise, you,

---

9   Psalms 131:3–4 LXX, OSB.

O children of the light, to praise the Lord of Hosts." For the night is a time when the sons of light arise for praise. "When we stand in the flesh before You, take away from our minds the sleep of forgetfulness, and grant us alertness, in order that we understand how to stand up before You at the time of prayer.... and win the forgiveness of our many sins."

When we practice the Midnight Prayer, we are granted grace and strength that makes up for all weariness and labor, which we think we would feel in praying at such a late hour. It is also known and ascertained by us that this hour has a special helping angel. As for staying up late for work, a person should not be deprived of few minutes at midnight, to participate with the sons of light in praising the Bridegroom.

While the Midnight Prayer symbolizes the culmination of watchfulness and meeting the Bridegroom, in reality, this actually happens partially in a way that makes the end of each day an attainment of the end[10] and victory by meeting the Lord.

The First Watch:

The prayers of the First Watch talk about the wise and foolish virgins and the life of watchfulness in preparation for meeting the Bridegroom. The gospel specifies that the coming of the Bridegroom is in the

---

10   That is, the goal.

middle of the night, to emphasize the importance of watchfulness to receive the Bridegroom. The most serious event is the standing of the foolish virgins outside and the shutting of the door to them.

In summary, the meeting that will take place with the Lord Jesus Christ is a meeting between the watching and waiting soul and the heavenly Bridegroom.

The Second Watch:

The prayers of the Second Watch talk about the repentant, sinful woman. Our meeting with the Lord at midnight is a meeting of a repentant person like the sinful woman.

Our meeting with the Lord at midnight is a meeting of a person who loved much as did the sinful woman.

Our meeting with the Lord at midnight is a meeting of tears—"and she began to wash His feet with tears."

Our meeting with the Lord at midnight is a meeting at the feet of the Lord—a meeting of contrition and worship.

Our meeting with the Lord at midnight is a pouring of ointment—that is, submission and dedication of our life to the Lord.

The last word which a soul hears in this meeting is, "Your faith has saved you; go in peace."

The Third Watch:

The Third Watch is the conclusion of prayers, where it talks about the submission of the whole life to the Lord. "Sell what you have, and give alms." "For where your treasure is, there your heart will be also." For the treasure of the Christian who is a sojourner on this earth is in heaven.

It then talks about the life of watchfulness and waiting for the Bridegroom. After that it talks about service and the work of the faithful and wise steward, whom his master makes ruler over his household.

And the last thing we hear in the Midnight Prayer is, "Come to Me you blessed of My Father, inherit the Kingdom prepared for you before the foundation of the world."

Yes, Lord, grant that we may be without fear in that Hour. Amen.

Times of Prayers and Their Quantity and Their Connection to the Cross of the Lord

The times of the prayers are linked to the sufferings of the Lord Jesus or to important events in a person's life. Therefore, they should be prayed at their appointed time, in order for us to remember what was accomplished for our sakes and what the Lord endured for us in these hours.

In the Prime Hour, we remember the Resurrection of the Lord early Sunday morning for our sakes.

At 9 a.m., we remember the coming down of the Holy Spirit, the crown of thorns and the scourging of the Lord for our sakes.

At noon (12 p.m.), we remember the crucifixion and passion of the Lord.

At 3 p.m., we remember the death of the Lord for our sakes, and so on.

Our love for Christ grows the more we meditate on the cross

A sinner merely standing before God the Father, clinging to the cross, entreating by the blood of Christ, sin falls away from him, and its judgement is lifted from him, and its curse passes away. Therefore, it is good for a person to hold a cross and kiss it frequently during prayer.

Let us be fully reassured that the moment we remember the cross of Jesus, it becomes a blessing for the whole hour. Not only that but it becomes a blessing for the whole day, the whole place and those around us.

The Quantity of Prayer

It is not required that we pray the hourly prayers completely in terms of quantity, but we can practice to commit to memory the gospels of the hours and to pray them at their respective times. We can then practice to memorize the litanies and pray them with the gospels at their appointed time. In time we can add a psalm as the grace of God aids us. Each of these prayers would only take a few minutes. However, we must pray Prime and evening prayers, according to our circumstances, as much as we can. For in these prayers, we go into our room and close our door.

The Importance of Prayer at its Appointed Time

This practice can save us from lukewarmness that can result from the length of time spent without prayer between the Prime and Compline Hours. On the contrary, the mere remembrance of the Lord even for a few minutes throughout the day, out of love and longing to be present with God, will fill our heart with spiritual fervor, protect us from temptation, and give us the grace of being in God's presence.

It is preferable that all this is practiced as a group, that is, a family gathering together to pray Compline, for example, or the Sunday School youth meeting in the church to pray Vespers and Compline; or when friends meet together throughout the hours of the day.

Lord, when will this spirit come true, that the Church may return to its original state—a Church of prayer.

"And they continued steadfastly ... in prayers" (Acts 2:42).

"So continuing daily with one accord in the temple" (Acts 2:46).

"Now Peter and John went up together to the temple at the hour of prayer, the ninth hour" (Acts 3:1).